# Keeping *the* Promise

## A Mentoring Program for Confirmation in the Episcopal Church

*Andrew D. Parker*

MOREHOUSE PUBLISHING

The excerpt from *Wishful Thinking: A Theological ABC* by Frederick Buechner, copyright © 1973 by Frederick Buechner, is reprinted by permission of HarperCollins Publishers, Inc.

**Morehouse Publishing**
P.O. Box 1321
Harrisburg, PA 17105

Morehouse Publishing is a division of The Morehouse Group.

*Cover design:* Corey R. Kent
*Cover photo:* CORBIS/Richard Hamilton Smith

ISBN    Mentor's Book: 0-8192-4113-X
        Confirmand's Workbook: 0-8192-4114-8
        ISBN-13: 978-0-8192-4114-6

*Printed in the United States of America*

03 02 01 00 99 98        10 9 8 7 6 5 4 3

# Contents

1. Starting Out ........................................................................................... 1

2. The Old Covenant: God and Israel ............................................... 3

3. The New Covenant: Jesus Christ and the Holy Spirit ............................. 6

4. Baptism and Confirmation ......................................................... 13

5. The Holy Eucharist ................................................................ 17

6. Spiritual Life ..................................................................... 22

7. Turning Points: Matrimony, Healing, Death ................................... 30

8. The Church ........................................................................ 33

9. Ministry ........................................................................... 37

# Section One

## Starting Out

**1. Mentor and Confirmand meet in an informal setting.**

Decide to go out to eat together, meet at one or the other person's house, or choose some other informal setting that is conducive to conversation. You might want to enjoy some activity together (like a sporting event or concert) as a way to start this time.

**2. Find out something about each other's background. Take notes to help you remember.**

Where were you born? Tell something about your growing-up years. What are some of your best memories? How about one of your sad memories?

Tell how you feel (felt) about school.

What is one thing you really like about your life today?

What is work like (or what will it be like) for you? What are your hopes for the future about your work life?

**3. Find out something about each other's faith experience.**

Have you always been a churchgoer? Always an Episcopalian?
What is important to you about being a church member?

Try to identify times in your life when your faith has changed.
How has it changed?

When did you first know you were a Christian?
Do you ever wonder about whether you really are a Christian?

**4. Draw a picture of how you imagined God when you were five years old.**

**5. Draw a picture of how you now imagine God to be.**

How has your understanding of God changed over the years?

**6. Talk about your expectations for this Confirmation process.**

What do you hope will happen during this time? What are you worried about regarding this process? Are you excited or nervous?

**7. Close your time together with each of you saying a short prayer asking God to be with you during this Confirmation preparation time, and thanking God for your partner in the process.**

**During the following week:**

Each of you should make a bookmark to exchange with your partner. On one side of the bookmark draw a symbol or picture representing something about yourself or your past life. On the other side, draw another symbol or picture representing God.

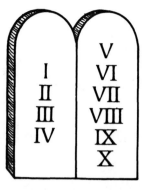

# Section Two

# The Old Covenant: God and Israel

**Before starting this section, exchange the bookmarks you and your partner have made and explain to each other what the drawings mean. Keep your partner's bookmark in your Bible as a reminder to pray for him or her.**

## 1. The Creation

The first chapter of Genesis tells how God created the heavens and the earth. Genesis 1:26-27 reads:

> Then God said, "Let us make humankind in our image, according to our likeness; and let them have dominion over the fish of the sea, and over the birds of the air, and over the cattle, and over all the wild animals of the earth, and over every creeping thing that creeps upon the earth." So God created humankind in his image, in the image of God he created them; male and female he created them.

What do you think it means to be created in the image of God?

What does this mean for how you view yourself?

What does it mean for how you view other individuals?

## 2. The Fall

**Read together Genesis 3:1-13, 22-24.**

What do you find interesting about this passage?

What does this story say about human nature and about the human condition?

Have you ever done something sinful (that is, something cruel or deceptive or unfair) without understanding why you did it?
Talk about a particular instance, if you can.

## 3. The Exodus

The book of Genesis tells how God tried time and time again to reach out to humanity, but we repeatedly turned our backs on Him and His will for us. In time, God began to form a relationship with one particular group of people, namely, Abraham and his descendants, who became known as the people of Israel.

The book of Exodus tells how this people became enslaved to the pharaoh (or king) of Egypt and how God raised up Moses to help deliver them. Moses threatened the pharaoh ten times with ten plagues because he would not let the Israelites leave Egypt. Pharaoh refused each time, and each time the plague came to pass. The final plague was especially deadly and killed the firstborn of every Egyptian family, but the families of Israel were spared. Their houses were "passed over" (Exod. 12:21-23). Then the Egyptians sent the people of Israel away "in haste" (Exod. 12:29-36).

**Read together what happens next in Exodus 14:5-31.**

If you had been one of the people of Israel, how would you have felt after passing through the Red Sea?

Jewish people today regard the escape from Egypt as perhaps the most important "formative event" in their history as a people. Why do you think it is so important for them?

Can we Christians consider this to be a part of our history too?

## 4. The Covenant at Sinai

After the Red Sea experience, the Lord led the people of Israel into the wilderness between Egypt and Palestine (which would become the land of Israel). At the mountain of Sinai, the Lord gave Israel his Law, summarized in the Ten Commandments, through the hand of Moses (Exod. 19:1-20:17).

**Read together the Ten Commandments, as written in Exod. 20:1-17.**
**Discuss what areas of life each of the Ten Commandments covers.**

Since we cannot fully keep the Ten Commandments, are they useful at all?

While still in the wilderness, the people of Israel agreed to obey the Commandments, and thus the Lord formed a covenant with Israel (a special relationship based on mutual promises). He would be their God and they would be his people.

We sometimes use the word "covenant" to describe a marriage or the relationship between a priest and his or her parish. How can these arrangements be called covenants? In what way might Baptism be a covenant?

# Section Three

# The New Covenant: Jesus and the Holy Spirit

The Apostles' Creed originated very early in the church, most likely in the second century (between A.D. 100 and 200). It was first used at Baptisms in a question-and-answer form; that is, the candidate for Baptism was asked, "Do you believe in the God the Father?" and the candidate answered, "I believe in God, the Father almighty, creator of heaven and earth," and so on. We still use the Apostles' Creed in this form today at Baptism and Confirmation (Prayer Book pp. 304, 416).

**1. Read the following section of the Apostles' Creed aloud together. Circle the words or phrases that stand out in your mind as interesting, unusual, or unclear and discuss them.**

a. I believe in Jesus Christ, _____

b. his only Son, our Lord. _____

c. He was conceived by the power of the Holy Spirit _____

d. and born of the Virgin Mary _____

e. He suffered under Pontius Pilate, _____

f. was crucified, _____

g. died, _____

h. and was buried. _____

i. He descended to the dead. <u>1 Pet. 3:18-19</u> , <u>4:6</u>

j. On the third day he rose again. _____

k. He ascended into heaven, _____

l. and is seated at the right hand of the Father. _____

m. He will come again to judge the living and the dead. _____

n. I believe in the Holy Spirit. _____


**2. What is the difference between saying "I believe in Jesus Christ" and saying "I believe that there is a Jesus Christ"?**


**To clarify the difference, try substituting the name of a friend for the words "Jesus Christ" in the two statements.**


**3. Certain phrases in the Creed point to key theological terms.**
   **Which line(s) from the Creed points to**
      **the Incarnation?**
      **the Resurrection?**
      **the Atonement?**

Note: <u>Incarnation</u> means "being in the flesh." It refers to the belief that God entered human life and became one of us in the person of Jesus Christ.

   <u>Atonement</u> refers to the belief that God, through the voluntary suffering and death of Jesus, removed the barrier of our sin, making it possible for our Creator and we, his creatures, to be "at one" (at-one-ment).


**4.** Incarnation, Atonement, Resurrection and the Holy Spirit are not simply cold, theoretical concepts. People sometimes speak of "experiencing" each of these.

a. "Incarnation" may relate to an experience of Christ in the world.
b. "Atonement" may deal with feeling the love Jesus showed by dying for us.
c. "Resurrection" describes having an experience of new life, or a new quality of life.
d. The "Holy Spirit" may have to do with experiencing God dwelling within us.

**Under what particular circumstances might someone experience**

    **a. Christ in the world (Incarnation)**

    **b. The love Jesus showed by dying for us (Atonement)**

    **c. Coming into a new life (Resurrection)**

    **d. God dwelling within him or her (Holy Spirit)**

**Do you feel that you have ever had an experience of the Incarnation, the Atonement, the Resurrection, or the Holy Spirit?**

**5.** We are able to affirm our belief in the Creed based on our own experience, the experience of people we know, and the experience of the church down through the ages (that is, the Tradition).

**What other authority do we have for believing the Creed?**

*During the next two to three weeks you will both need to read on your own the Gospel of Luke, chapters 1-9 and 19-24, and the book of Acts, chapters 1 and 2. Decide on a reading schedule, so that you will both be reading at the same pace. (Suggestion: if you read one chapter a day, then you will finish in 17 days.)*

**6. As you read Luke and Acts, fill in the blanks for question 1 with the Bible verses that support each particular line from the Creed.**
For example, the first line, which indicates that Jesus is the Christ, is supported by Luke 2:11 (where the angel tells the shepherds that Jesus "is born this day in the city of David, a Savior, who is Christ the Lord"). Also Luke 9:20 (where Peter declares that Jesus is "the Christ of God"). Supporting Bible verses for line 9 have been provided for you, since these are not in Luke or Acts.

**7. As you read the Gospel of Luke, write down:**

• **The sayings of Jesus which give you comfort or hope**

• **The sayings of Jesus which disturb or challenge you**

**8. Jot down your comments, reactions, and questions as you read each chapter. Discuss your notes at your weekly meetings.**

Luke 1: _____
_____
_____
_____
_____
_____

Luke 2: _____
_____
_____
_____
_____
_____

Luke 3: _____
_____
_____
_____
_____
_____

Luke 4: _____
_____
_____
_____
_____

**Luke 5:** _____
_____
_____
_____
_____
_____

**Luke 6:** _____
_____
_____
_____
_____
_____

**Luke 7:** _____
_____
_____
_____
_____
_____

**Luke 8:** _____
_____
_____
_____
_____
_____

**Luke 9:** _____
_____
_____
_____
_____
_____

**Luke 19:** _____

_____

_____

_____

_____

_____

**Luke 20:** _____

_____

_____

_____

_____

_____

_____

**Luke 21:** _____

_____

_____

_____

_____

_____

_____

**Luke 22:** _____

_____

_____

_____

_____

_____

**Luke 23:** _____

_____

_____

_____

_____

_____

Luke 24: _____
_____
_____
_____
_____
_____
_____

Acts 1: _____
_____
_____
_____
_____
_____

Acts 2: _____
_____
_____
_____
_____
_____

**9. Think back through the major events in the portion of Luke which you read and make a rough outline of Jesus' life.**

_____
_____
_____
_____
_____
_____
_____
_____
_____
_____
_____

## Section Four

## Baptism and Confirmation

### 1. Investigate your own Baptism.

Can you remember when you were baptized?

How old were you?

Ask your parents what they remember about your Baptism.

Where was it?

Was it in an Episcopal church or another denomination?

Was it a private or public ceremony?

Who was there? Who was the minister?

How did *you* handle it all?

Find out whether you or your family have any photos, or certificates or pew bulletins, from your baptism and bring them to your next meeting.

### 2. How would you describe what Baptism is?

**Compare your description with the first sentence on page 298 of the Prayer Book.**

**Since Baptism is "full initiation" into the church, then who is eligible to receive communion?**

3. Read together the three "Do you renounce . . ." questions on page 302, which are asked of people being baptized (or of their parents). What does "renounce" mean? What would it mean for you if you renounced "Satan . . . evil powers . . . and sinful desires"?

Read together the next three questions. What would it mean for someone's life if he or she answered "I do" to these questions?

Imagine that you were never baptized and now you are thinking over what Baptism means. Could you answer "I do" to the three questions?

4. In Section Two, a covenant is described as a special relationship between two parties based on mutual promises. We considered several examples of covenants— between God and Israel, between wife and husband, a priest and his or her parish.

**As part of the Baptismal Covenant (Prayer Book, pp. 304-305), what five promises do we make?**

**Which of these promises is the hardest for you to keep?**

**Which is the least difficult for you?**

5. Read together the "Thanksgiving over the Water" (pp. 306-307) and the prayer after Baptism (top of p. 308). Write down God's promises to us in Baptism. (The promises are reflected in Romans 6:1-5; 1 Corinthians 12:12-13.)

6. In the Episcopal church we (like most, though not all, other Christians) baptize infants to show that God's saving work is for everyone, even if a person is too young to understand it. We do not wish to exclude children from God's family. Furthermore, in the New Testament we find examples of whole families being baptized together (Acts 11:14, 16:15, 16:33).
**When a baby is baptized, how are the renunciations and promises made?**

**What additional promises do the parents and godparents make?**

**7.** Some churches practice Baptism by immersion (dunking), others by pouring (with a dish or the hand), others by sprinkling (with the fingers).
**Which methods are permitted by the Prayer Book?**
**Which method would you prefer if you were being baptized?**


**Does Baptism "work" regardless of the method used?**
**In other words, can you be saved whether you are immersed, poured upon, or sprinkled?**


**What does Romans 10:9-13 say about this issue?**


**8. What is Confirmation, in your thinking?**


**How does your answer compare with the description in the first paragraph on page 412 of the Prayer Book?**


**9. Look at this table, which compares the Baptism and the Confirmation rites.**

| BAPTISM | CONFIRMATION |
| --- | --- |
| Presentation (p. 301) | Presentation (p. 415) |
| Examination: six questions (p. 302) | Examination: two questions (p. 415) |
| Question to the Congregation (p. 303) | Question to the Congregation (p. 416) |
| Baptismal Covenant<br>  a. the Apostles' Creed (p. 304)<br>  b. Promises (pp.304-305) | Baptismal Covenant<br>  a. the Apostles' Creed (pp. 416-417)<br>  b. Promises (p.417) |
| Prayers for the Candidates (pp. 305-306) | Prayers for the Candidates (p. 417) |
| Thanksgiving over the Water (pp. 306-307) | |
| Baptism by Water (p. 307) | Confirmation with Laying On of Hands (p. 418) |
| Concluding Prayer (p. 308) | Concluding Prayer (p. 419) |
| Anointing with Oil (p. 308) | |
| Welcoming Newly Baptized (p. 308) | |
| Passing of the Peace (p. 308) | Passing of the Peace (p. 419) |

Why do you think the rites are so similar?

Why do you think there is no "Welcoming" in the Confirmation rite?

10. Have you learned anything new about Confirmation since you started this program? How does the prospect of being confirmed make you feel? Do you have any qualms or hesitations?

11. Remember to discuss the reading that you have done so far in Luke.

## Section Five

## The Holy Eucharist

Holy Baptism and the Holy Eucharist are the "great sacraments of the Gospel" because they were given to us through Jesus Christ as recorded in the Gospels. Although these two sacraments are distinct, they are closely tied together. In the early church, the newly baptized always received their "first communion" immediately after their Baptism. Many of the same themes considered in Baptism arise again with the Eucharist; for example, Christ's death and resurrection, the forgiveness of sins, and new life.

**1.** Jesus Christ instituted the Eucharist on the night before his death when he celebrated the Jewish Passover meal with his disciples. (For the origins of the Jewish Passover, turn again to Exodus 12:21-27.)

**Read about the Last Supper in Matthew 26:26-30.**

**What things, persons, or words or actions in this account of the Last Supper do we find in our Sunday celebration of the Holy Eucharist?**

**2. What important information does Acts 20:7 give us about the practice of the first Christians?**

**3. Why do you think Christians have been so persistent about "the breaking of the bread" for so many centuries?** (A clue: 1 Corinthians 11:23-25).

By joining in the Eucharist and by partaking of the body and blood of Christ we share in Christ's death and resurrection, his sacrifice and atonement. (Remember atonement? See Section Three, Question 3.) In this way we receive forgiveness for our sins, continual strengthening of our union with Christ and with one another, and nourishment in eternal life.

**4.** By the year A.D. 375, the simple "breaking of the bread" had developed into the more involved "Holy Eucharist," very much like our Eucharist of today. This word *Eucharist* literally means "thanksgiving."

**What are we giving thanks for in the Eucharist?**

**5.** The Holy Eucharist is sometimes described as a drama in two acts. The first act is called "the Word of God" and the second act is called "the Holy Communion." Take a look at the Outline on page 20 to see how it is divided in two.

During the first act, the word of God is presented in the Lessons from the Bible, in the sermon, and in the Creed. We then <u>respond</u> to God's word by the Prayers of the People and by passing the peace.

The second act, "Holy Communion," has a four-part structure based on verses such as Matthew 26:26 (also Mark 14:22, Luke 22:19): Jesus (1) took bread, (2) blessed it (or gave thanks), (3) broke it, and (4) gave it to the disciples.

**Referring to the Outline, when are the bread and wine taken up?**

**When are the bread and wine blessed (or given thanks over)?**

**When is the bread broken?**

**When are the bread and wine given to the people?**

**6. Do you feel that you have ever sensed Christ's presence in the Eucharist?**

**7. What to you is most important about the Eucharist?**

**8. Don't forget to talk about your continuing reading in Luke and Acts.**

# OUTLINE OF THE HOLY EUCHARIST (RITE TWO)

## A. THE WORD OF GOD

1. Introduction
   *
   Opening Dialogue: "Blessed be God . . ."
   Collect for Purity: "Almighty God, to you all hearts are open . . ."
   Canticle: Usually the *Gloria*: "Glory to God in the highest . . ."

2. Collect of the Day (a prayer for the particular Sunday)

3. The Lessons (usually three, interspersed with Psalm and hymn)

4. The Sermon

5. The Nicene Creed

6. The Prayers of the People (with confession of sin)

7. Passing of the Peace

## B. THE HOLY COMMUNION

1. The Offertory (People and priest offer bread, wine, alms to God.)
   *
2. The Great Thanksgiving
   *Sursum Corda*: "Lift up your hearts . . ." (dialogue)
   Proper Preface (appointed for the season of the year)
   *Sanctus*: "Holy, Holy, Holy . . ."
   Prayer of Consecration
   The Lord's Prayer

3. The Fraction (Celebrant breaks the bread): "Alleluia, Christ our Passover . . ."

4. The Distribution of Bread and Wine
   *
5. Closing
   Postcommunion prayer
   Blessing
   Dismissal: "Let us bless the Lord . . ."
   *

* Indicates a point where hymns may be added.

# Optional Information

Making the sign of the cross, bowing the head, and genuflecting (bending the knee) are frequently seen in church. These "manual acts" reflect the fact that we worship with our bodies as well as with our minds and voices. Whether you choose to perform some or all of these manual acts should depend upon your own sense of worship and the custom of your congregation.

## During the Liturgy

Sign of the Cross—reminder of Baptism in the name of the Trinity
- At the Opening Acclamation: "Blessed be God, Father, Son, and Holy Spirit."
- At the announcement of the Gospel—three small crosses with thumb on forehead, lips, and chest, "that the Gospel might be in my head, on my lips, and in my heart."
- At the end of the Creed: "The resurrection of the body."
- At the Absolution: "Have mercy on you."
- Following the *Sanctus* : "Blessed is he who comes."
- Before receiving the bread, then before receiving the wine.
- At the Blessing: "The blessing of God Almighty, the Father, the Son, and the Holy Spirit."

Bow Head—to show reverence to God, to Christ, or to his sacrifice on the cross.
- When the processional cross passes your pew.
- At beginning of the Gospel: "Glory to you, Lord Christ."
- At end of the Gospel: "Praise to you, Lord Christ."
- In the Creed during "by the power of the Holy Spirit, he became incarnate from the Virgin Mary, and was made man."
- At the *Sanctus* during "Holy, holy, holy, God of power and might."

## In the Church Building

Reverence the altar (bow) when passing before it, as when entering the pew.

Genuflect when passing before the consecrated bread and wine, if these are reserved in an aumbry (a box in or on the wall near the altar).

## Section Six

## Spiritual Life

**1. Talk a little about prayer. What is prayer?**

**Do you ever pray? When?**

**Why do people pray? Why do *you* pray?**

**2. Someone once defined prayer as "communication with God in a relationship of love." Why do you think this person used the words "communication with God" instead of "talking with God"?**

**Why is "a relationship of love" an important aspect of prayer?**

**3. Many Christians find that they need a prayer time or "quiet time" every day (or most days). If you have a daily prayer time, talk about that. If you don't, then try it for (at least) the next five days, using the format on the following pages. Find a quiet, private place and spend five to ten minutes each day.**

**4.** The word "grace" can be difficult to grasp, but it is central to the Christian faith. Grace is the love and the favor and the power that God freely gives to us. The life, death, and resurrection of Jesus Christ show forth God's grace. We are saved through God's grace. God works in our hearts by his grace, strengthening us, enlightening us, and forgiving us. The Sacraments of Baptism and the Eucharist are means of grace (though they are not the only means of grace).

Frederick Buechner writes:

> Grace is something you can never get but only be given. There's no way to earn it or deserve it or bring it about any more than you can deserve the taste of raspberries and cream or earn good looks or bring about your own birth. A good sleep is grace and so are good dreams. Most tears are grace. The smell of rain is grace. Somebody loving you is grace. Loving somebody is grace. Have you ever *tried* to love somebody?

**Grace is too slippery a word for easy definition. So just close this book and call out words that you associate with the term "grace."**

**Can you think of any time that you experienced God's grace?**

**5.** Different people respond to God's grace in different ways, such as through the following disciplines:

- Service: helping those in some need
- Bible study: drawing nearer to God through his Word
- Reading spiritual or devotional books
- Fasting: going without food to "make space" for God
- Meditation: listening to God via some "object," such as a leaf, a painting, or a scripture
- Keeping a spiritual journal: reflecting on one's life and God's work in it
- The rite of Reconciliation: confessing one's sins to God in the presence of a priest (in the *Book of Common Prayer* pp. 446-452)

**Have you ever done one (or more) of these? What was your experience?**

**Are you interested in finding out more about any of these disciplines? How could you go about learning more?**

**Why do you think we talk about these various disciplines in terms of God's grace?** (Ephesians 2:8 can help you with this one.)

**If you have finished your reading in Luke and Acts, then you should complete Questions 6-9 in Section Three.**

# Day One

**Silence:** for a few moments, to remember that you are in the presence of God

**from Psalm 51** (say slowly and prayerfully)

> **Have mercy on me, O God, according to your loving-kindness;**
> > **in your great compassion blot out my offenses.**
> **Wash me through and through from my wickedness**
> > **and cleanse me from my sin.**
> **Create in me a clean heart, O God.**
> > **And renew a right spirit within me.**
> **Cast me not away from your presence**
> > **And take not your Holy Spirit from me.**
> **Give me the joy of your saving help again.**
> > **And sustain me with your bountiful spirit.**
> **Open my lips, O Lord,**
> > **And my mouth shall proclaim your praise.**

## Conversation with God

Take several minutes just to talk with and listen to God. Tell God where you are, mentally or emotionally. Tell God whom you are concerned about and what your own needs and troubles are. Confess anything that may be weighing heavily on you. Give thanks to God for what he gives you, for what he does for you, and for just who he is.

## Closing Prayer

**O Lord, support us all the day long, until the shadows lengthen, and the evening comes, and the busy world is hushed, and the fever of life is over, and our work is done. Then in your mercy, grant us a safe lodging, and a holy rest, and peace at the last. *Amen.***

**Notes:** Write down anything in your prayers that struck you as important.

# Day Two

**Silence:** for a few moments, to remember that you are in the presence of God

**from Psalm 73** (say slowly and prayerfully)

> Truly, God is good to Israel,
>> to those who are pure in heart.
> But as for me, my feet had nearly slipped;
>> I had almost tripped and fallen;
> Because I envied the proud
>> and saw the prosperity of the wicked.
> When my mind became embittered,
>> I was sorely wounded in my heart.
> I was stupid and had no understanding;
>> I was like a brute beast in your presence.
> Yet I am always with you;
>> you hold me by your right hand.
> You will guide me by your counsel,
>> and afterwards receive me with glory.
> Whom have I in heaven but you?
>> and having you I desire nothing upon earth.
> Though my flesh and my heart should waste away,
>> God is the strength of my heart and my portion for ever.

## Conversation with God

Take several minutes just to talk with and listen to God. Tell God where you are, mentally or emotionally. Tell God whom you are concerned about and what your own needs and troubles are. Confess anything that may be weighing heavily on you. Give thanks to God for what he gives you, for what he does for you, and for just who he is.

## Closing Prayer

Almighty and eternal God, so draw my heart to you, so guide my mind, so fill my imagination, so control my will, that I may be wholly yours, utterly dedicated to you; and then use me, I pray, as you will, and always to your glory and the welfare of your people; through our Lord and Savior Jesus Christ. *Amen.*

**Notes:** Write down anything in your prayers that struck you as important.

# Day Three

**Silence:** for a few moments, to remember that you are in the presence of God

**from Psalm 104** (say slowly and prayerfully)

> The trees of the Lord are full of sap,
> > the cedars of Lebanon which he planted,
> In which the birds build their nests,
> > and in whose tops the stork makes his dwelling.
> The high hills are a refuge for the mountain goats,
> > and the stony cliffs for the rock badgers.
> You appointed the moon to mark the seasons,
> > and the sun knows the time of its setting.
> You make darkness that it may be night,
> > in which all the beasts of the forest prowl.
> The lions roar after their prey
> > and seek their food from God.
> The sun rises, and they slip away
> > and lay themselves down in their dens.
> Man goes forth to his work
> > and to his labor until the evening.
> O Lord, how manifold are your works!
> > in wisdom you have made them all;
> > the earth is full of your creatures.

## Conversation with God

Take several minutes just to talk with and listen to God. Tell God where you are, mentally or emotionally. Tell God whom you are concerned about and what your own needs and troubles are. Confess anything that may be weighing heavily on you. Give thanks to God for what he gives you, for what he does for you, and for just who he is.

## Closing Prayer

O merciful Creator, your hand is open wide to satisfy the needs of every living creature: Make us always thankful for your loving providence; and grant that we, remembering the account that we must one day give, may be faithful stewards of your good gifts, through Jesus Christ our Lord. *Amen.*

**Notes:** Write down anything in your prayers that struck you as important.

# Day Four

**Silence:** for a few moments, to remember that you are in the presence of God

**from Psalm 139** (say slowly and prayerfully)

> Lord, you have searched me out and known me;
> > you know my sitting down and my rising up;
> > you discern my thoughts from afar.
> If I say, "Surely the darkness will cover me,
> > and the light around me turn to night,"
> Darkness is not dark to you; the night is as bright as the day;
> > darkness and light to you are both alike.
> For you created my inmost parts;
> > you knit me together in my mother's womb.
> I will thank you because I am marvelously made;
> > your works are wonderful, and I know it well.
> My body was not hidden from you, while I was being made in secret
> > and woven in the depths of the earth.
> Your eyes beheld my limbs, yet unfinished in the womb;
> > all of them were written in your book;
> > they were fashioned day by day,
> > when as yet there was none of them.
> How deep I find your thoughts, O God!
> > how great is the sum of them!
> If I were to count them, they would be more in number than the sand;
> > to count them all, my life span would need to be like yours.

## Conversation with God

Take several minutes just to talk with and listen to God. Tell God where you are, mentally or emotionally. Tell God whom you are concerned about and what your own needs and troubles are. Confess anything that may be weighing heavily on you. Give thanks to God for what he gives you, for what he does for you, and for just who he is.

## Closing Prayer

O God, you made us in your own image and redeemed us through Jesus your Son: Look with compassion on the whole human family; take away the arrogance and hatred which infect our hearts; break down the walls that separate us; unite us in bonds of love; and work through our struggle and confusion to accomplish your purposes on earth; through Jesus Christ our Lord. *Amen.*

**Notes:** Write down anything in your prayers which struck you as important.

# Day Five

**Silence:** for a few moments, to remember that you are in the presence of God

**from Psalm 116** (say slowly and prayerfully)

> I love the Lord, because he has heard the voice of my supplication,
> > because he has inclined his ear to me whenever I called upon him.
> The cords of death entangled me; the grip of the grave took hold of me;
> > I came to grief and sorrow.
> Then I called upon the Name of the Lord:
> > "O Lord, I pray you, save my life."
> Gracious is the Lord and righteous;
> > our God is full of compassion.
> The Lord watches over the innocent;
> > I was brought very low, and he helped me.
> Turn again to your rest, O my soul,
> > for the Lord has treated you well.
> For you have rescued my life from death,
> > my eyes from tears, and my feet from stumbling.
> I will walk in the presence of the Lord
> > in the land of the living.
> I believed, even when I said, "I have been brought very low."
> > In my distress I said, "No one can be trusted."
> How shall I repay the Lord
> > for all the good things he has done for me?
> I will lift up the cup of salvation
> > and call upon the name of the Lord.
> I will fulfill my vows to the Lord
> > in the presence of all his people.

## Conversation with God
Take several minutes just to talk with and listen to God. Tell God where you are, mentally or emotionally. Tell God whom you are concerned about and what your own needs and troubles are. Confess anything that may be weighing heavily on you. Give thanks to God for what he gives you, for what he does for you, and for just who he is.

## Closing Prayer
Lord Jesus Christ, you stretched out your arms of love on the hard wood of the cross that everyone might come within the reach of your saving embrace; So clothe us in your Spirit that we, reaching forth our hands in love, may bring those who do not know you to the knowledge and love of you; for the honor of your Name. *Amen.*

**Notes:** Write down anything in your prayers that struck you as important.

## Section Seven

## Turning Points:
## Marriage, Healing, Death

**1. Follow up on the last session.**

**Were you able to have your five days of prayer time?**
**What was the experience like?**

**Did having a prayer time influence the rest of your day in any way?**

**Write a prayer for a concern you have about the world.** Here are some possible subjects: for peace, for the environment, for the poor or homeless, for the sick, for the dying, for the oppressed.

**2. The Prayer Book calls Holy Matrimony "a solemn and public covenant between a man and a woman in the presence of God."**
**What makes marriage a covenant?**

**3.** Unlike Baptism, Eucharist, Reconciliation, or any other sacramental rite, marriage is not something peculiar to Christians. Why do you think that this natural institution has been taken into the church?

**4.** If you ever do marry, what would you want marriage to be like?

**5.** Have you ever attended a healing service? Did anything surprise you? What was the purpose of the healing rite?

**6.** James 5:14 reads "Is any among you sick? Let him call for the elders of the church, and let them pray over him, anointing him with oil in the name of the Lord."

**What similarities do you see between this Scripture and the healing service?**

**7.** The liturgy for the burial of the dead is an Easter liturgy. It finds all its meaning in the Resurrection. Because Jesus was raised from the dead, we, too, shall be raised. (Note that the color for a burial service is always white, as for Easter.)

**Does this mean that it is unchristian to grieve for someone who has died?**

**8. What does "eternal life" mean to you? Has the way you have pictured eternal life changed as you've grown older?**

**9.** Episcopalians distinguish the "two great sacraments of the Gospel," Baptism and Eucharist, from the five "other sacramental rites," namely, Reconciliation, Confirmation, Matrimony, Unction (Anointing) of the Sick, and Ordination.

**Why do we make this distinction?**
Clue #1: Think about where these rites originated.
Clue #2: Compare the second question on p. 858 with the second question on p. 860 in the Prayer Book.

**Why do you think that the burial of the dead is not a sacrament?**

## Section Eight

## The Church

**1. Read again what happens in Acts 2:1-17 and 2:36-47.**
NOTE: Pentecost, a Jewish festival that falls fifty days after Passover, recalls the giving of the Law to Moses on Mount Sinai.

**2. This first Pentecost following the resurrection of Jesus has come to be known as the birthday of the church. Why would we say that the church was "born" on this day? In other words, what things happened then that still happen in the church today?**

**3.** The church (the community of the New Covenant) is frequently called "the Body of Christ" in the New Testament. Romans 12:4-8 (TEV) says this:

> We have many parts in the one body, and all these parts have different functions. In the same way, though we are many, we are one body in union with Christ, and we are all joined to each other as different parts of one body. So we are to use our different gifts in accordance with the grace that God has given us. If our gift is to speak God's message, we should do it according to the faith that we have; if it is to serve, we should serve; if it is to teach, we should teach; if it is to encourage others, we should do so. Whoever shares with others should do it generously; whoever has authority, should work hard; whoever shows kindness to others, should do it cheerfully.

**What does it mean for the people of our congregation all to be different parts of Christ's Body?**

**Do you see the gifts mentioned in Romans in any of the people or the activities of our parish (those gifts of speaking God's message, serving, teaching, encouraging, giving, holding authority, showing kindness)?**

**God gives to people many talents, abilities, character traits, and deep desires that are expressed in the Body of Christ. What gifts do you bring (or could you bring) to the church?**

**4. Talk about the Vestry (or Bishop's Committee) meeting which you attended together. You may need to refer to the notes you took at the meeting.**

**How was the Vestry meeting different from other organizational meetings? How was it the same?**

**What interested you most about the meeting? What business took up the greatest portion of the time? What was the main goal of the meeting? Did the group strike you as acting like "the Body of Christ"?**

**5. Review the current church budget. What does the budget tell you about the church's priorities?**

**Were you surprised by anything you found in the budget?**

**Does it seem as though we spend too much or too little money on any particular item?**

**6. Discuss how you would respond to a person making this statement: "I think somebody can be a good Christian without being part of a church."**

_____ is part of:

| | No. of people | No. of units |
|---|---|---|
| The Diocese of _____ | _____ | ____ parishes and missions |
| The Episcopal Church in the USA | 2½ million | 123 dioceses |
| The Anglican Communion | 70 million | 28 provinces (countries or groups of countries) |

The Anglican Communion is the fellowship of churches across the globe which are descended from the Church of England. The largest provinces (in order of size of membership) are England, Nigeria, Australia, United States, Southern Africa, and Uganda. Each province has its own Book of Common Prayer, although the books are very much alike. The Archbishop of Canterbury calls all the Anglican bishops together every ten years for the Lambeth Conference in London.

Anglicanism is the third largest Christian Communion (or denomination) in the world. Only the Roman Catholic and Eastern Orthodox Communions are larger.

# THE EPISCOPAL CHURCH MAP

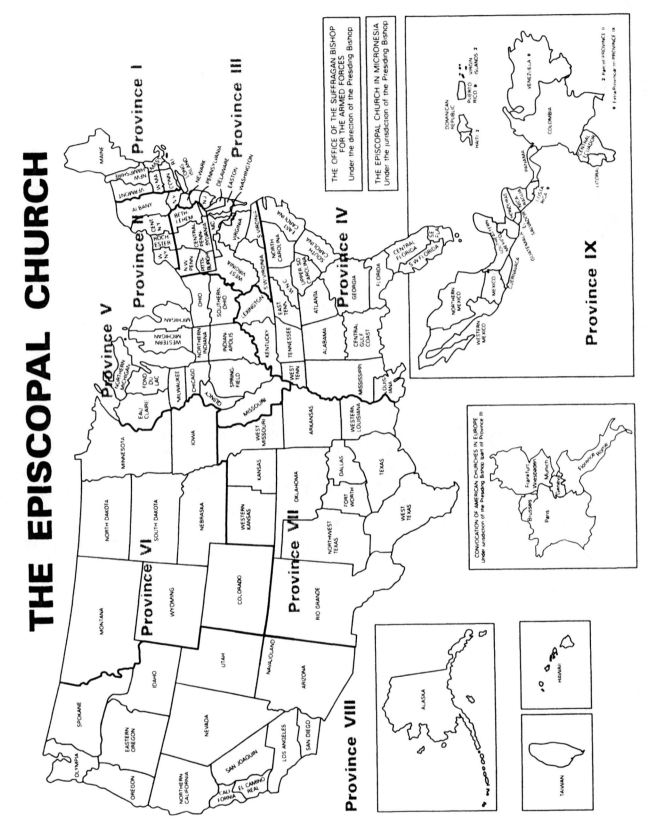

*Map used by courtesy of the Executive Council.*

# Section Nine

# Ministry

**1.** Last session we considered
- How the church began (the outpouring of the Holy Spirit at Pentecost),
- What it is (the Body of Christ, the community of the New Covenant), and
- Something of how it is actually organized (in the Vestry, in the budget).

We now turn to what the church does, its mission and ministry. The Catechism in the Prayer Book states that the mission of the church is "to restore all people to unity with God and each other in Christ," and that this happens when the church through all its members "prays and worships, proclaims the Gospel, and promotes justice, peace, and love" (p. 855).

**In what place (or places) does the mission of the church proceed?**

**2. Two helpful categories are the "Church Gathered" and the "Church Scattered." What would you guess is the difference between these two aspects of the church?**

**3. Given these two arenas for ministry, the Church Gathered and the Church Scattered, do you believe that one is more important than the other? Which one?**

**4. What is the relationship between the Church Gathered and the Church Scattered?**

The following Postcommunion Prayer (p. 366) may help with your answer:
> Almighty and everliving God, we thank you for feeding us with the spiritual food of the most precious Body and Blood of your Son our Savior Jesus Christ; and for assuring us in these holy mysteries that we are living members of the Body of your Son, and heirs of your eternal kingdom. And now, Father, send us out to do the work you have given us to do, to love and serve you as faithful witnesses of Christ our Lord.

**5.** The Catechism states that the ministers of the church are "lay persons, bishops, priests and deacons" (p. 855).
**How can lay persons be called ministers?**

**Why do you think that lay persons are mentioned first?**

**6. Is the primary arena for the ministry of lay persons in the Church Gathered or in the Church Scattered?** (Consider the number of hours an average lay person spends at the church building.)

**7. Read again the five Baptismal vows (pp. 304-305 in the Prayer Book). Where do you now have opportunities to fulfill those vows? Where might you in the future have such opportunities?**

**8. Tell each other about a time when someone ministered to you. Then tell about a time when you ministered to another person.**

**9. Think back to the special act of ministry which you engaged in for this program. What were you expecting before you went? Were your expectations accurate, or not? What part of the experience did you like and what did you not like? Why should the church be engaged (or not be engaged) in this sort of work?**

### A Prayer at Confirmation

Grant, Almighty God, that we, who have been redeemed from the old life of sin by our baptism into the death and resurrection of your Son Jesus Christ, may be renewed in your Holy Spirit, and live in righteousness and true holiness; through Jesus Christ our Lord, who lives and reigns with you and the Holy Spirit, one God, now and for ever.

AMEN.

CPSIA information can be obtained at www.ICGtesting.com
Printed in the USA
LVOW11s0921011013

354833LV00002BA/22/P